Believing without seeing

It happens to the best of us. It drives you nuts. You sip your morning coffee and bite the frozen pizza, turn on streams from questionable websites, and suddenly the computer gets overloaded with window after window as cellular multiplication renders the system useless. Yes, it happened to me. That too, in the much-awaited inaugural game of the 2011 World Cup between Bangladesh and India where I missed out my favorite player - Virender Sehwag - blowing the brains out of bowlers of my favorite team -Bangladesh - with his epic 175. But, that wasn't the first time. There were many other occasions where I was a step away from putting my neck on railtracks, just for a fix of my team in action.

No. 10 - Signal loss, computer crash
As the computer gets overloaded with multiple windows, I start panicking. The irritable buffer syndrome was tolerable; but a complete shutdown of system? I figured it would take 20 minutes for a full system recovery. I would lose 20 minutes of the match, but it would be still worth it.

Alas! After 20 minutes of excruciating wait, it seemed that I made an error in setting up the LAN connection. Encore! I automatically hit the 'Power' button, F10, F10, F10 and the familiar subroutine of system recovery began for a second time.

So 40 minutes into the game, I have not gotten a single, uninterrupted feed. What's in store next? Codec doesn't work. Besides, I would badly need an anti-virus shield to further prevent breakdown. At any rate, I was in a catch-22 situation, for to get codec I must have anti-virus software, but due to Safe Mode, I cannot install many components. I panicked. I stormed out of my house, waited fifteen minutes for bus with additional twenty minutes en route to finally reach the public library for a stream. And all these times, I was swearing at myself for not test driving the online video links beforehand. But it was an unfortunate day. I logged on and then I realized that the library does not supply headphones. Luckily a family friend of ours lived nearby. Huffing and puffing when I finally reached their house, it would take another patient fifteen minutes before the door would be opened, as the elder daughter mistakenly would mistake my heavy pounding on the door for the work of a miscreant.

No. 9 - The violin match
Inspired by the late Sherlock Holmes, I always wanted to learn violin. I loved the classical electrical fusion of the instrument. And my father was anxiously looking to find me a hobby as a form of music therapy for depression. So obviously I did not want to miss the class. But my mind cut the Gordian knot that is the ubiquitous Dhaka gridlock before coming home to learn Bangladesh had defeated Zimbabwe by one wicket to win the series 3-1. I also learned that Dr. Muhammad Yunus was awarded Nobel Prize. Two good news in one day!

No. 8 - The wedding problem
Do I go to a wedding or witness a live online feed of Mohammad Ashraful scoring a big hundred on his Test comeback? I could stay at home but I had to take my mother, and as everyone knows, mom 'cannot drive freeways'. As the venue was about 17 miles away I was the chosen victim. So with iPad in hand we drove down to Haveli's Indian Cuisine. They had some Indian songs on TV, and no wifi. Thus I had to resort to annoying my friend for his cellphone every five minutes to casually see Ashraful off across the milestone bridge.

No. 7 - The insult
After a quarrel with my mom, I had gone to my cousin sister's house for refuge. As luck would have it, she had an invitation to someone's place for a party, and I had to tag along as an uninvited guest. To make matters worse, I was promptly relegated to the kids' room, while the adults clinked champagne glasses (or was it sherbet?), and partook in grapes and kebab. And there I was, a Bangladesh cricket expert fan, being tickled and teased, and forced to borrow a kid's laptop to log in for the live feed, as the cell phone fee was piling up already. And that was when Tamim Iqbal was tearing England apart with a ferocious innings, and threatening to get to 100 in a session.

Tamim would become the quickest Bangladesh player to pass 1000 Test runs, reaching his half-century from 53 balls, but he slowed down thereafter.

No. 6 - In transit
This time it was by sheer chance that I was forced to miss the match. Flying from Bangladesh, transiting at Singapore and Japan, I had to keep tabs on cricket through whatever means were available. As I logged onto Banglacricket.com, the very refreshing banner titled "Bangladesh in British Isles 2010 - First win against England" brightened up my moment. Bangladesh had won a nail-biter by five runs. I had no need to wield the cumbersome, squeaky mouse anymore, to browse at a snail's pace while paying a premium. I had got what I wanted and logged off like a boss.

No. 5 - Train ride from Sylhet to Dhaka
During one of Tamim's masterclasses on that 2010 trip to England, I had the pleasurable misfortune of experiencing Sylhet's rapturous beauty. Only problem - no electricity, leave alone internet. And when the cell phone did manage to pick up signal it was outside the periphery. I eventually returned to Dhaka courtesy a scenic train ride, with my cousin Ananta giving me text updates. His promptness made the train ride a lot more enjoyable than it would have otherwise been.

No. 4 - Load-shedding
Aftab Ahmed was on fire as Bangladesh chased 309. End of over 19 (6 runs), Bangladesh 110/1 (199 runs required from 31 overs, RR: 5.78, RRR: 6.41. And then it happened - the inevitable load-shedding. We decided to head back home from my aunt's house to our residence in Banani where we were hoping that the electricity would thrive. By the time we got home and turned on the TV, Bangladesh had proceeded to reach a rotten position. They would go on to lose by 23 runs against Pakistan.

No. 3 - Dilemma, dilemma...
It was day I became a US citizen. My loving mother planned a Chinese dinner outing to celebrate. It was also the day Bangladesh were playing Australia in Darwin. I could not possibly say no to my mom. While we gorged on the food, I was a little disappointed that I couldn't fully enjoy the moment. We skipped dessert and headed home only to see Bangladesh in a familiar position of collapse.

No. 2 - Asia Cup slip
Who can forget Shahadat Hossain bowling a messy spell, and then arriving at the crease to face the last ball, and not being able to get the winning boundary? I barely got a sliver of the screening of the Asia Cup final as I had an important epistemology class to attend. I was way behind the minimum attendance requirement, so there was no question of missing this session. Later, I patiently stood in the queue to enter the computer lab. This time I even had headphones. Alas, there was no glory.

No. 1 The genesis
Back to where it all began. Here I was, a Bangladeshi in South Africa, supporting my team against Kenya in the 1997 ICC World Cup qualifier final via Voice of America and British Broadcasting Corporation radio stations, relaying only bits and pieces of the match report from
Kuala Lumpur in Malaysia. It was all worth it when the first piece of good news around Bangladesh cricket was relayed to me - they'd won the rain-curtailed last-ball thriller. This was the beginning. My dad would proudly proclaim to his teenager son: "A dangerous team is coming to world cricket. That team is Bangladesh."

A serendipitous encounter with a Tiger

In the earlier months of this current year on a rainy day a curious event took place which no one could have foretold.

It began on a rainy day. Imagine the din and hustle in a noisy gridlocked traffic at Dhaka in Bangladesh. We were stuck toggling AC on and off and suddenly the driver Musa received a phone call from his boss ergo my uncle to provide transportation to my mother in Dhanmondi. It would have been really a long commute so the driver immediately wanted to take off leaving us stranded us in the street. So after he left we got out and it started drizzling mildly.

My cousin Ananta is a strange fellow and he is recurring partner in crime in many of our adventures of Bangladesh cricket. It's just a matter of tragedy that recently he suffered stroke but in spite of the fact that he got shocked, his giant bear like cuddly frame (as the ladies call him) was barely stirred. He could climb Everest at will even now with his confidence. But pragmatism before pride and even at babysteps we know it'd be a far walk. So we decided to take the rickshaw and reached the Grameen office for him to purchase tickets for the upcoming Sri Lanka game.

Right after we reached at the ground floor parking lot of the building my cousin's mobile died. He panicked, because he had the code for ticket in it. Unfortunately no one had the charger, but hey it's Bangladesh where anything is possible. So we decided to take a detour and at the same time lunch somewhere.

Again we had to take a rickshaw and his healthy figure (read obese) would hardly offer me any comfort or any hope in the rickshaw but I patiently endured the lack of leg or body space muttering expletives at him under my breath. We got off and gave the rickshawala a few tuppence and decided to walk. We found a mobile seller who incidentally carried the charger and decided not to charge us.

As I pushed the door only to find out that you have to pull it (or vice versa?) I smeared their floor with mud and I wanted to slap myself for not only making a mess of it but also because they were doing the charging for gratis which could've easily gone against us because of the fumble.

We wanted to kill the time with lunch so Ananta remarked: "We will feast on the first place we see." Apparently it was Pizza Hut and after fifteen minutes or so we feasted on the scrumptious thin crust meal.

It was time to go back, so we picked up the phone, thanked the gentleman with some tip and headed for Grameen office. It was a short queue and then Ananta found out that the code doesn't work and he may have to get a different end - North or South - I forget. So he made the call and got the code and got a different end.

And then suddenly Ananta cried out: Apni Tiger na? (Aren't you the Tiger?)

I turned around to see what was Ananta possibly on. Turned out it was a middle-aged gentleman in black t-shirt with short receding hair and goatee. Ananta ribbed me with his elbow: It's the Tiger, don't you get it?

"Oh you must be Tiger Liton from Mirpur!" I couldn't contain my delight being in front of a celebrity star struck as ever.

"Tiger Milon," he corrected me.
"Yes yes Tiger Milon. Milon bhai."

After we exchanged pleasantries I told him how I blog sometimes for Cricinfo and would love to do a write up on him. I wanted to give him space and respect privacy but asked him few questions. He did mention whether it took 40 minutes or 2 hours to paint himself up as a Tiger in yellow costume. Honestly I don't remember.

What I do remember was the fact that he was an incredibly down-to-earth humble man. In spite of the fact getting recognized he offered to take photos with fans (as he did with us) and was incredibly polite. He explained how he was a rare disorder which prompted Bangladesh Cricket Board to give him free tickets and expedited entrance. At this, I was immediately aghast with shame inside my body because once I wanted to write in a Fan Following how there is no creativity as he was being a copycat of the original Tiger, Shoiab. I was also immediately moved by the compassion shown by BCB. So much goes on behind the scenes, yet it is so easy to sit behind the computer screen thousands of miles away and make judgements with few keystrokes.

Turned out Milon bhai wanted a different end of the stand and that's exactly what my cousin had. Serendipitously it worked out as they exchanged the tickets with Milon bhai repeatedly saying in a polite tone "Are you sure you don't want this?" He couldn't believe his eyes that he would got the right end of the stands.

Neither could we. On our way back, we were talking about this strange coincidence and Ananta mused: "What are the odds that this would happen?"

As Brad Pitt's character pointed out in Benjamin Button: " Sometimes we're on a collision course, and we just don't know it. Whether it's by accident or by design, there's not a thing we can do about it."

The driver had to receive the call from my uncle (Mama) at certain point to make the decision for an U-Turn. At that instance, the rain would have to start drizzling for us to stop walking and consider a rickshaw. Only by a stroke of luck, the cell phone or mobile had to die at the basement of Grameen office for us to reconsider matters. As we did so, we had to find that certain mobile store where I would smear the floor with mud. It'd follow shortly after a pizza meal in a nearest Pizza Hut store after my cousin would remark "Let's stop at the nearest food place" when we could've easily eaten biryani or something else. And it would only have to be certain time to make that pizza ready before we would go back to the mobile store to pick up the charged phone. After we did so, only by matter of luck that the mobile would reveal he did not get the right code for ticket and my cousin had to call the number. But he would get a different end, and then coincidentally after the chance encounter with Tiger Milon everything would work out.

You cannot possibly arrange such things.

'One down, Bangladesh strikes'

'One down, Bangladesh strikes!' It has a certain vibe to it. It sends down psychological fear and chills down spine of opponents. 0-1, the asymmetrical score has certain aesthetic to it. Zero runs on board, and a wicket has already fallen.

Most often than not the obverse has been the case. Bangladesh found themselves tangled up in all sorts of problem where nought for three is not so unfamiliar. Chaminda Vaas World Cup hattrick and the recently concluded Test against Zimbabwe when team was three down for zero are two such prime examples.

Since the inception of Bangladesh into cricketing arena, they have been at the brunt of attacks and bludgeonings , litany of humiliations, lampoons in terms of records, losing streaks and of course, their trademark collapses of lineup that fades away dimly like astral dust.
However a moment comes in a bowler's career when all his acumen and tradecraft honed over the years culminates to a point - that defining cusp of the universe- when the known laws of physics break down, and that's when the paranormal begins.

A supernova of explosion. A burst of creative energy. And - stumps rattled. These are the tales of those explosive moments which have been horrific for opponents. Bangladesh shone, be it for milliseconds, to rock the opposition.

A. Gurusinha 0 c. Aminul Islam b. Saiful Islam

An earlier victim was Asanka Gurusinha. Perhaps his first name encapsulates the forthcoming. The second match of Pepsi Asia cup was played at Sharjah. I wasn't at the stadium, but for those few Bangladeshis present there on 6 March, 1995 it must have been a sight to behold.

Imagine the likes of Jayasuria, Aravinda da Silva, Mahanama and Ranatunga playing against Bangladesh and then...out of nowhere - comes Saiful Islam to dismiss Gurusinha for duck. I can easily concoct a false visual memory of an entire nation exploding looking at this vignette. Sri Lankan players mentioned at this time were like cogs and wheels of a bulldozer. They were taking the world by storm and then this happens. Of course Sri Lanka would rebound strongly with a Jayasuria 50 to win by 107 runs. But hey, the deed has been done.

Senanayaka 0 c. Akram Khan b. Gholam Nousher

Rewind back to Asia Cup about four years ago. It's the eve of 1991; victory month for Bangladesh. Third match of the tournament being held at Calcutta. One cannot be blamed for not remembering this match. But ask Gholam Nousher. Surely he must! For it is another of those rare occasion when a Bangladeshi would take a prize scalp of a heavyweight with the score reading... nought for one.

And this time? It's Bangladesh on top.

Patterson 0 lbw b. Hasibul Hossain

His nickname is Shanto, which in Bangla means the 'quiet one'. But this man was anything but shy in the very first over of '99 World Cup match against Scotland.This same match Khaled Masud pilot would return to pavilion for a duck facing only 9 balls. Bangladesh would post a modest 185 which they would go on to defend. However, the icing of the match must have been when Shanto removed Patterson for a duck as the scorecard would read 0 for 1. Subtle, soft, and a silencer. The best would be saved for last when later on in the tournament Bangladesh would defeat Pakistan.

Wasim Jaffer 0 b. Mashrafe Mortaza
Wasim Jaffer 0 c. Habibul Bashar b. Shahadat Hossin

It's a day Jaffer would love to forget for he bagged a pair in the first Test on May 2007. Mashrafe's delivery is every fast bowler's delight, more so because it happened on the first ball of a Test match.That too bowled. And Bangladesh would draw the match.

Poonia 0 c. Aftab Ahmed b. Mashrafe Mortaza

Given a target of 279 runs to fetch, Scotland would easily succumb to pressure losing Poonia for a duck in the second ball. Mashrafe would strike again on the fourth one of the over to remove Brown. This time bowled. Bangladesh would go on to win convincingly by 146 runs.

Cricket is a funny game they say. There are times when a player would be a crowned man-of-thematch from a losing side. There are awards for spirit-of-the-game. Now although these vignettes have not been match winning per se, they are etched forever in fans' and bowlers' mind alike, because just for a brief second, they give the sublime insight of what a person is capable of summoning when the time is ripe.

And one such showdown was the ICC Trophy Final between Kenya and Bangladesh in 1997. As millions patiently waited for the match to start, they would not be disappointed. Dressed in white after a smooth flowing run up with brisk hair Saiful Islam would bowl the fourth ball. The ball did not appear to pitch fast but it was deadly accurate. A thwack followed by a banana split of two stumps falling in opposite directions. The familiar death knell.

Bangladesh would then be part of the elite nations after winning the match despite a Kenyan

century.

That was the inception. Now that is something you don't see quite often!

Attempting the impossible

Belgian surrealist painter René Magritte suffered from ennui or existentialist boredom. He sought out to think of "unthought like thoughts" and a cricket fragment, being art, should strive to do just that- shatter intellectual paradigm, toppling the zeitgeist by pulling the rug under the audience making the game unboring. That's what art does after all! It shocks and awes. Now, I always wanted to pen the Great American Cricket Novel so here I am attempting the impossible through some figment of fiction through synopsis of plots:

Scoring ~40 runs in an over

Like Einstein, nevermind that I am nowhere standing on the genius's shoulder, I always wanted to read God's mind and pen the ultimate cricket script. Hell, in an interview I even read that one of my team's favourite batsman, Tamim Iqbal, dreams of a scenario where 60 runs are needed off 2 overs and he scores them for his team. Is this impossible? Imagine, how cool would it be to see that on Bangladesh soil a player scores about 40 runs in an over- just enough to push the envelope. Imagine demon seizing the batsmen as wides, no balls galore followed by sixes and fours and fours and sixes at the right dosage in punctuated equilibrium to evolve the collective nous of cricket fans. Just imagine.

And then there are times when I would pen how a player has...

Gone berserk!

Imagine a Bangladeshi scoring Rohit Sharma or Shane Watson like sixes. Sixteen. Fifteen. Fourteen. It doesn't matter. He is possessed. Whether it be street cricket or village, his whirlwind onslaught would not only shatter bungalow glasses but the perceived paradigm of what a soft spoken Bangladeshi should be. Yes, he'd be my ultimate weapon as the protagonist.

And while we have our Bellerophon, we also need a chimeric incubus in the form of a bowler who takes wickets at will.

Five wicket haul....in a single over

Yeah, it's about time we raise the bar. Enough of mediocrity trumpeting bowlers who go home in their secure lab to sing their swan song of fifers living up to to some classical symphone of 'class' and 'waltz'. Nay, it's John and Johnny Cage style breaking the brick wall with cry of silence. I would compose in my novel the juggernaut who takes five wickets in a single over. Not a single spell or a quota, but a single over, guys.

First Bangladeshi to score triple century

That's my dream. And if he does it I'd make sure he would do so in the most efficient manner possible. Surgically, methodically and with fluency of a storm trooper.

Nine-wicket club

Nine wickets or even ten in a match is boring. But, taking nine wickets in an innings isn't. And that's just what I want from Bangladesh. Too often we think of a team from a least developed country to be underachieving chumps who don't have the guts to dream big lest what other cares. But why? This sort of mediocrity appalls me and in my perfect plot I envision not only players from my country who takes 9 wickets regularly but does so with...

Complete and utter domination

...where even his team mate batsmen buttresses him with a gargoyle like innings of 200 plus runs. And while we get into beast-mode, it is only apt that a country where we see so much poverty, strife, poor health and political turmoil, that nothing could tarnish the echt of the sport:

Human spirit

Nothing can destroy human spirit whether devilry chops off costly arms and legs like Robert Frosts "Out out-" or even when a human is boggled with mundane chores of maintaining livelihood. My hero would have no feet to support him and this one armed bandit would make sure that you can vilify'm but one thing you cannot do is ignore'm demanding double take from you.

Culled from various sources, it happens that my power of imagination is really not that strong enough. For every aforementioned matter delineated can be vouched to be true sprung from Bangladesh in various obscure minor matches or domestic leagues. So perhaps that is the rewarding part of the sole journalist in a stadium or a spectator atop a water tank tower.

Alauddin Babu conceded 39 runs in an over to Hamilton Masakadza on my homeground. Perhaps not a record to be proud of but wait.

Ziaur Rahman holds a nice little spot in Wisden for his brutal 15 sixes in his century stand against Central Zone. And his nemesis that we clothed up, Al-Amin Hossain actually took five wickets in a domestic Twenty20 over. First Bangladeshi to score a triple century? None other than the violent but often times slow paced Raqibul Hasan who gave us a brief glimpse of his avatar by revealing the godly face of Shiva in mayhem and destruction! Be it picnic cricket! And my country has her fair share of 9 wicket takers in the guise of Abdur Razzak, U-19 Siddikur Rahman Shawon, and even Abu Haider who gave just the boost for total domination of a sapling and touch-me-not Qatar team when Soumya Sarkar would score his not-so-official 209.

Folks, these may be some no name not so hotshots but these obscure faces and records are just what's needed to pull the rug under the feet to unsettle things a little and make life a bit more unboring. Just the right dosage of chaos is needed to introduce to lift the human spirit above realms of mediocrity. For when, an unknown kid in Bangladesh with no feet and one arm has beastly Scarface mentality to say that "I can bat like Tamim and smack sixes outside the boundary-line; I can turn the ball like Shakib and get wickets;and I can field like Nasir and restrict the opposition from scoring" perhaps that's what's needed in these day and age for the ultimate volte-face in not only Bangladesh, but World Cricket.

C'est n'est pas cricket?

You decide.

Photographic memory and six Rubel Hossain

Rubel Hossain for some reason put a hex on me. For some reason I seem to have a near photographic memory when it comes to his bowling feats. No, not super eidetic imagery as to what time and day it was, what over he was bowling, what was the headline of that day, or the final score. No. None of that extraneous stuff. I remember the feeling, the ecstasy, the sheer exultation and euphoria his effect seem to have from the Svengali bowling.

Now Rubel Hossain is not someone you want to meet at the back alley in the middle of night. Stocky, well built- almost that of rapper 50 cent's feature- and statuesque ivory black chiseled figure he looks morel like a boxer than a fast bowler. A first of his kind. Add to that his aggressive slingy bowling, sometimes wayward, sometimes short-pitched, but when it lands in the zone, like a sniper crosshair's he seems to go right for the perfect kill.

I do remember the odd anecdotes how he loves motorcycles, how after a domestic hat-trick spanning two overs, he didn't know of his accomplishment, how he said he mimics Malinga after growing up in a tape tennis environment. Yes, I do remember these odd facts. But below are those moments in time which mere words cannot describe or encapsulate. Going by a memory witness to his testament, these are some of those glimpses of his efforts and effects which left indelible impression upon my memory forever. These are the moments when the avatar landed for darsan when his fury, vision and wrath that was unleashed.

1. A blinder of a catch

First time I saw Rubel Hossain in flesh and blood was oddly enough in my first time at stadium. I remember Fahmim Ferdous, a friend of mine, was sitting to my right, and my cousin Shatil. Fahmim was wearing a Lamborghini yellow t-shirt that I remarked. I am not much of Test person but when it comes to Fan Following and ego searching in Cricinfo website, nothing presents a grander chance than this. Test match is an acquired taste where mammoth totals are cumulative and work of labor instead of flash in the pan effects. Yet this flash of the pan moment, this flash of genius, this insight, this inspiration, this haiku burst of theta brainwave was forced me on my feet.

I didn't know what happened. There was no replay in stadium. Rubel was near out stands, and I am sure I remarked in Bangla to some effect: Why leak so many runs? But suddenly a batsman went full monte and it was a six. No scratch that. Someone interrupted. A bird? A plane? No Rubel Hossain plucked the ball off the sky in a blinder. In Bangla we call it: "lufey niyeche". Literally, grabbed it. Not sure who it was, probably Kane Williamson, but when Rubel jumped about a feet high, took the catch - an otherwise sure six- it took a moment for me to process what was going on. It was as if the dumbstruck feeling an avid birdwatcher feels when she sees a rare warbler or a tern.

Fahmim was the first to react: That's wow moment of the day.

2. Match winning debut

False memories are dangerous and it to mask the sheer delight of his debut's match winning performance I always thought it was a fifer till I checked and it turned out to be a four wicket debut. Rubel has done the damage. Why noteworthy? Because Bangladesh lost to Zimbabwe and Sri Lanka and was definitely out of the tournament. Man of the match was Shakib al Hasan whose controlled and gritty hard hitting of 92 runs took us home to qualify for the final. But it was indeed Rubel's deliveries that went straight into the heart of the matter.

I was at my Rina Apa's house. A cousin of mine. Dad and I watched the first session where he took the wickets and he thoroughly enjoyed it. I remember how my cousin's husband -Saif bhai- chided his son, my nephew, Sajid why he wasn't praying and I knew that he was a bit annoyed from the noise interference to his studies so he scolded him. However, I secretly knew, he was envious of father-son bond between us, and he took is a cricket lover. (Love you Saif bhai!) So the platform has been set, but that's where Rubel made a mess.

3. Fall from grace

With a low total to defend, Bangladesh would totter the batting lineup at 6/5. First ball was a run out wicket, I later checked. Nazmul and Mashrafe shared the first four amongst them. The memories are bit saccadic and staccato since it was late at night, Mom was sleeping, and I didn't want to wake up so I was following Paltalk commentary. But I had to get up 5 times when wicket fell with headphones around my ears with lights and computer monitor turned off. I had to even sleep awkwardly with my head facing the near end of computer so as to be tethered to the feedback.

Rubel would make a mess and get a thrashing by Murali who guided the team to a win at death. As I check, he leaked 20 runs in an over.

Rubel was no longer my hero.

4. Kyle mills delivery

Over and over, so many times I rewinded the Kyle Mills delivery on Youtube that ended New Zealand's plight for first Banglawash. I was living in my own rented room. I was watching on laptop in sharpshooter position. As if I was watching the match through my lenscope because that is totally what it felt like: Assassination. A perfect yorker, a thud, wicket falls, Mills bowled...and the entire stadium e-rupts!

What a feeling!

Later I found out Ian Pont reveal in a forum that that week before Rubel was practicing at net and then after Ian placed a coin saying that would signal the end, Rubel would go forth to landing the ball pitch perfect.

But I could be wrong.

5. The wicket that wasn't

This one I don't remember the details but it turns out Braithwaite was the victim in West Indies tour of Bangladesh in 2011. I got a brief flash that stumps were shattered, and indeed two uprooted. But irony of all ironies! It could have been - it seems 8 for 1 - if not for the no ball. I could only imagine how gutted he must have been felt for it was a gem of a delivery. I mean two wickets knocked out. What else do you want as a Bangladesh viewer? But it was a no ball. And I don't think he got a wicket that day. Or did he?

6. Violence and larceny

Perfect symmetry is of nature's. I returned from a rain interrupted first ODI of New Zealand and Bangladesh. Now Bangladesh drew the Test series. So the match was evenly poised for anyone to take the game after rain interruption. I left the stadium ruing the fact of a Fan Following wasted. But it was another of those father-son bond.

The first time I leaped in joy in cricket was when a Pakistani bowler would a take a wicket to dismiss Australia out of the world cup. That was the cold night I remember when my Mom was served separation papers as right I jumped in joy my Mom's grave face entered the room. A mere child, I immediately knew what was wrong. And ever since then, I always felt guilt of being too euphoric.

However, Providence is the brutal judge who will force you to face the facts. This time when I was watching with Dad, my sixth sense told me something was up. The game was even-Stevens at the cusp and then what began could duly be called "violence and larceny".

First wicket. Sheer unbridled euphoria inside me. I was sitting next to Dad who was more circumspect and didn't react after Rubel's first ball. Second one, gone!! An entire psychic earthquake swayed inside me and I was moved but no, I wanted more. Another. My loud voice thundered. Dad was unswayed. Another!! I could feel it. I could project it. I could visualize it. Like a North American shaman I could manipulate reality. I knew it it's gonna happen. I could feel it. This time my sixth sense too didn't lie. And then I jumped. I jumped in joy and sheer delight. It wasn't contrived. I did not plan to leap in air; it was a karmic retribution in the most apt sense to liberate me from the trauma I experienced the other night. If the first leap of faith brought tears from parents' separation, this sheer joy of delight was nothing but marriage made in heaven. And this time I didn't even have to support Pakistan, but Bangladesh. My Bangladesh! Even Dad cracked a smile.
Hat trick.

I mean the feeling. It cannot be put into words. But they are forever etched in my mind's photographic plate. I could recall those events, run it, rewind it and fast forward it like a mind movie. And they are with me forever and wherever I can take them to.

I am not trying to eyewash the readers thinking these are not elaborations of photographic memory. As the deeper down the rabbit hole you go, more and more questions will always be asked? How many runs did he give? What was the colour of his shoes? Who was at the commentary box? Well, then why not at what angle the light cast shadow? Or for that matter, the decibel of the volume of crowd?

Eidetic memory doesn't exist. What exists are extremely powerful receptor for lifelong containment of these indescribable feelings and sheer euphoria. And if that doesn't suffice, if not Ramayana, I can always quote this own article of mine verbatim!

Duel set as Bangladesh aim to dominate

"The duellists demands satisfaction. Honour, for him, is an appetite." -The Duellists (1977)

Once upon a time during a battle, a Japanese general decided to attack even though his army was greatly outnumbered. Although he had no doubts that they would win, his soldiers were not so sure. After praying at a religious shrine, the general took out a coin and said that after he tosses the coin, if it lands heads then they will win and if otherwise, than they will lose leaving it to destiny. The coin landed heads. The buoyant soldiers were so overjoyed and filled with confidence that they attacked the enemy brutally and were victorious. When the battle ended, a lieutenant remarked: Nobody can change destiny.

"Yes", the general smiled showing the coin.

It had heads on both sides.

The story is especially ironic because of the fact that Bangladesh lost to Sri Lanka in a coin toss in the recently concluded Asian Games for a bronze medal. Luck, it goes without saying, hasn't been especially fair to the Tigers. A Caribbean T20 literally washed out, bad umpiring in various forms, a loss despite a Taskin's superb debut – all contributed to hardly any memorable event this year. However, luck also favours the prepared mind, and this time Bangladesh tigers are prepared.

As Bangladesh is set to take part in a duel against their familiar rival Zimbabwe, records shows that Zimbabwe is extremely strong on paper when it comes to deciders in Test. But that is in tainted context as Bangladesh began their full-fledged career only recently while the likes of Flower brothers were in the squad in the pioneer days. Thus, it would be rather naive to read between the lines going solely by statistics.

The story of Bangladesh cricket and Zimbabwe is of contrasting complexion. Eyeballing the squad reveals that Zimbabweans are in the late 20s and early 30s while Bangladesh is full of new, young and exciting prospects. Nineteen year old leg spinner Jubair Hossain is one such example who has been included in the Test squad. Zimbabwe who has been playing a long time before than Bangladesh meanwhile produced a Hamilton Masakadza 178* versus Kenya, the fourth highest ODI scorer Charles Coventry with 194*, former player Eddo Brandes, the oldest one to take a hat-trick. Such records although doesn't dictate outcome of game as gleaned from various contexts but do speak volumes about their rich heritage. On the contrary Bangladesh performance over the years has been sporadic and inconsistencies.

In 2013, Zimbabwe defeated Pakistan in the second test drawing the series 1-1 which was their third victory against Pakistan and their only fifth against Test playing nations excluding Bangladesh. Although the milestone victory is undoubtedly a sweeter moment in their chart, it is a brand new page for both rivals in the upcoming series.
Shakib-al-Hasan will make a return and Bangladesh will have a new ODI captain Mashrafe bin Mortaza. Bangladesh will aim to dominate with full force because Zimbabweans are their nearest

rival in the ICC ranking of Test teams where the former is at the rock bottom and Zimbabwe at ninth. While Heath Streak the Zimbabwean bowling coach is optimistic as ever.

In Ridley Scott's 1977 debut directing film "The Duellists", there is a scene where the protagonist after getting severely wounded in the chest laments to his love interest that he could have gone on with fighting. At one point as he was about to sneeze, she urged his mind to focus on something else and screamed "Describe honour!" "Honour is indescribable! Unchallengeable..." but he could not control himself and finally sneezed to tremendous pain. This has more ramification than ever because ultimately whether it be a fencing duel, arm wrestling or a matching of wits in a chess, it is the mind-set that controls the destiny.

Bangladesh have faced their arch-rivals on numerous occasions but failing to stamp their authority on them. Just like the hero found his muse and his raison d'etre, his purpose for life to swivel around and fight to the hilt in a bloody duel, each player must do so, that is find their inner calling, forgetting the past, focus on the present series and hope for the best in the upcoming World Cup tournament.

Ultimately when a player dawns that jersey, nothing is more honourable than playing for his own country at his home ground.

Regal return for Shakib Al Hasan

Anything that can go right, will go right. Converse to Murphy's law, this a direct testament to the first day of the first Test of Zimbabwe tour of Bangladesh. Barring a few misfields and dropped catches, and the wicket of Tamim Iqbal late in the day, it goes without saying that the day belonged to Bangladesh. Everything proceeded in clockwork fashion from a first over wicket to wickets falling at regular intervals with tidy spells in the bowling department as well as a revelation in the form of a debutant leg spinner Jubair Hossain. However, the hero of the day was Shakib Al Hasan with his triumphant return taking 6 for 59 to restrict Zimbabwe to 240. In the process, Shakib became the first and only Bangladeshi to take 5 wicket haul against every Test playing nations he played against.

First blood

Although the spotlight has been on Shakib's heroics, it was Shahadat Hossain's wicket in the very first over that started Zimbabwe downfall. After being dispatched for four in the first ball of the day, Shahadat would return with a fast delivery in the fifth ball to see off Vusi Sibanda with an edge to keeper Mushfiqur Rahim. Hossain, who made a return after a long hiatus, was visibly over the moon.

Revelation of the day

Despite Jubair Hossain being another player overshadowed by the experienced and senior luminary Shakib, the former made his presence known with many variations in his repertoire including flippers and wrong un's in stock. After Zimbabwe won the toss and elected to bat first, there was plenty of purchase for the spinners and Jubair, not afraid to give flight and toss the ball in the air, took full advantage taking two crucial consecutive wickets of third and fourth batsmen. He is young and remains an exciting prospect if he can be properly mentored.

Zimbabwe retaliation

The Zimbabweans had but themselves to blame as they were gifting their wickets with lofted shots succumbing to pressure and showing hurried intention. Briefly they put up a resistance with third and fourth wicket partnerships with Sikander Reza scoring a stubborn half-century before falling prey to Jubair. Other than Reza's fifty there is not much to write home about, as Bangladeshis were equally culprit that included two misfields from Tajiul Islam and Al-Amin resulting in a dropped catch and a four that really should not have been the case at this level of cricket. Later in the day a superb delivery by Panyangara bouncing to take Tamim Iqbal off guard would earn the guests but little solace in a spin dominated match.

Tale of two dead balls

Umpire would call a dead ball after a kite interrupted the ongoing proceedings when the batsman would leave playing a ball. Another one being in the Bangladeshi innings after Mominul Haque would dispatch Nyumbu for four but umpire Dharmasena signaled dead ball as a short leg fielder was moving during bowling.

A one man show

Shakib's sixth wicket to remove the final man was merely an icing as he already bagged enough to achieve the rank of being the to take five wicket hauls against every Test playing nations he played against. The left-armer, who is not unfamiliar with laurels, being the leading wicket taker for Bangladesh with 122 Test scalps, continued to show his merit by bowling the right deliveries with just enough variations. Recently he served a two and a half month ban from international cricket, and any doubts to his capabilities or contributions should be put to rest. While another young spinner Taijul Islam chipped in with the debutant Jubair, the ever experienced Shakib with his tidy spells and economy remained a class apart from the rest and dominated solely taking the center stage.

What lies ahead

It was unfortunate for Al-Amin who is a hard working cricketer to remain wicketless and Bangladesh may be ruing the loss of Tamim's wicket putting 27 runs on board. They would need to remain wary of Zimbabwe who will be eager to bounce back after first day's bruise because for Bangladesh throwing away opportunities is nothing new and nothing would be more devastating for the Tigers to see history repeat itself in the form of all too familiar collapses that they have seen before.

Bangladesh squad: Tamim Iqbal, Shamsur Rahman, Mominul Haque, Mushfiqur Rahim (c/wk), Shakib Al Hasan, Mahmudullah, Shuvagata Hom, Taijul Islam, Jubair Hossain, Shahadat Hossain, Al-Amin Hossain

Zimbabwe squad: Sikandar Raza, Vusi Sibanda, Hamilton Masakadza, Brendan Taylor (c),Craig Ervine, Elton Chigumbura, Regis Chakabva (wk), Tendai Chatara, Tafadzwa Kamungozi, John Nyumbu, Tinashe Panyangara

Bangladesh script dramatic win

A Taijul 8 wicket haul. A meager target of 101 runs to win. And...nought for three for a start. The third day at Mirpur had all the right dosage of a thriller. Bangladesh did not win any matches in any format of the game in this year, but when they finally did in the first Test against Zimbabwe, every runs and every wickets were hard earned with lessons to be taken away from the match.

The mystery pitch

Of course any match that is wrapped up within three days of a Test is bound to ask the question what sort of pitch it could have been. Zimbabwe would win the toss and elect to bat first and set a first innings lead of 240 runs. Bangladesh, although, would move past the lead by 14 runs, they would be disappointed not to reach the ideal 300 plus runs that was talked about in press meeting when taking on to bat. On the third day, a total of 17 wickets would fall giving plenty of movement in a gloomy and overcast conditions at Mirpur fuelled by a spirited Zimbabwe comeback. Although ultimately Bangladesh would win, one could not help but wonder about the unfriendly home conditions set by the curator.

Taijul's record 8 wicket haul

Slow left arm spinner Taijul Islam was on fire as he would decimate Zimbabwe in the earlier innings. In the process, he would be the first Bangladeshi to have a best figure of 8 for 39 for a historical record. He would also etch his a name as the third slow left armer possessing the best figures in an innings following Rangana Herath's recent 9 wicket haul and Johnny Brigg's 8-fer in 1889.

0 for 3

Following Taijul's fiery spell with a target of 101 runs to win on a tricky surface, Bangladesh would make a wobbling start with 0 for 3. Tamim would be dismissed in a similar fashion of first innings giving a catch to slip, following Shamsur's duck bowled by Panyangara. Matters would get worse when Mominul would also fall to Chigumbura for another duck. At that stage, Bangladesh did not put any runs on board and were reeling at 0/3. Shakib and Mahmudullah would try to steady the ship with confident shots, but as wickets fell it was up to Mushfiqur Rahim and the hero of the day Taijul Islam to finish the game.

Zimbabwe pace attack

Full credit must be given to the venom of the Zimbabwean seamers for testing the batsmen aided by bounce and movement. Chigumbura bowled exceptionally well who would take 4/21 after making early breakthroughs with Panyangara. Zimbabwe was never out of the game and till the last shot of the day kept gnawing at the opponent and crawling back with threat.

Man of the moment

It was a poetic justice after all for Taijul Islam to make the winning shot. With four runs to win he would pull Chigumbura to backward square leg for the boundary. The young left armer was exuberant and would kiss the ground after scoring the winnings runs.

What lies ahead

As Bangladesh leads the series 1-0 and go to Khulna for the second test they must be wary of the top order dilemma since middle or later order cannot afford to provide the getaway card everytime. They must also sort out issues with selection of squad as Al-Amin was wicketless in the first Test with Shamsur Rahman and Shuvogato Hom making hardly any contribution. Shakib who found his muse in the first innings and got a lone scalp in the third, would be the key as well as the Jubair Hossain and Taijul who has been fresh of breath air for the team.

Score

Zimbabwe 240 and 114

Bangladesh 254 and 101/7

Bangladesh won by 3 wickets

Me, my Bapi and Bangladesh cricket

Back in 1958 I was in Zurich, and there I met an extraordinary man by the name of Karlfried von Dürckheim. He was a former German diplomat who had studied Zen in Japan and when he came back after the war, he opened a meditation school and retreat in the Black Forest. And he said, "Well, I'll tell you what, a lot of my work has to do with people who went through spiritual crises during the war." And, he said, "You know, we all know when a person is in an absolutely extreme situation, and they accept it, there is a possibility of a natural satori." And that's what I mean when I was explaining that when one gets to an extreme - that is to say to the point when you realize there is nothing you can do about life, nothing you can not do about life, then you're the mosquito biting the iron bull. Well, so in the same way he said, "Look. You heard a bomb coming at you, you could hear it whistle, and you knew it was right above you and headed straight at you and that you were finished. And you accepted it. And suddenly, there was a strange feeling that everything is absolutely clear. You suddenly see that there isn't a grain of dust in the whole universe that's in the wrong place. That you understand completely, absolutely, totally what it's all about, cause' you can't say what it is.

- Alan Watts

Cricket transcends from being just a sport when it ends up building a bond between father and son. Both of us are completely different people: He prays five times a day, while I am agnostic. He keeps fit, and me? Well, I am just fat. He prefers formal attire; while I like white t-shirts and jeans. He graduated with a Masters in Public Administration and I am a college dropout. He has travelled to at least 40 countries while I get my fill of the world by collecting stamps. We share the same genes but we are two different souls. But, as Steve Jobs said, it is only when you reflect back upon your life and when you connect the dots that you begin to see patterns.

Bangladesh beat Pakistan by 62 runs in the 1999 World Cup

Our story begins in South Africa. Like every kid, my mind ran amok with what I wanted to be when I grew up. One day it was a 6'4" renaissance man from Harvard, or a magician like David Copperfield. But I desperately wanted to be a cricketer and never got the support from Bapi, as I call him. Bapi worked at the embassy and he would urge me to focus on studies, often highlighting Anil Kumble's engineering degree. So when I left him for the US, I wept like a little infant.

I followed the game via Cricinfo before the era of Sopcast. Naturally when Bangladesh pulled off a stunner - controversy or not - I was ecstatic. Then one day I travelled to South Africa to meet Bapi. We roamed here and there, sometimes to Italy or Egypt or Zimbabwe bordering Zambia in a river boat cruise and Windhoek. We visited a Bangladeshi friend's house and as chance would have it, they had the VHS tape of the Pakistan-Bangladesh match. "Lagaan! Lagaan! Khela lagan!" My Bapi could not ontain his delight, which roughly translates to "Put it on! Put it on!" Although I do not remember much of it, but I do recall someone telling me how fat I was. But that moment is one of the most cherished of my life. It began my bond with Bapi.

Bangladesh beat Australia by five wickets in June 2005

I had to return to California soon after the South Africa trip, but I occasionally went back to Bangladesh to visit Bapi, who moved back to the country. Then one day he had to visit India for work but I got to tag along. So after visiting Humayun's tomb, Agra Fort and Qutb Minar and enjoying the local flavour, I returned to hotel.

Bapi took one bed and I took the other with Robert Ludlum's Lazarus on my lap. As he flipped the channel, highlights of Mohammad Ashraful's innings came up. This was years after I ran away from home, but I can still recall how Bapi said the adrenaline from watching that game left him unable to sleep.

Bangladesh drew with India in the Chittagong Test of 2007

I was hospitalised for mental instability, but things did get better after I was discharged. Bapi and I grew fonder of each other. Bapi, by the way likes his records. So when highlights of the Test

came on television and Mashrafe got Wasim Jaffer with a jaffer off the first ball of the match, Bapi was up on his feet. "Bowled!" he cried out. "May be Bangladesh won this that is why they are showing it," he said. I chuckled. It was actually drawn as I would later find out.

These are some of my most cherished moments. I roll them over and over in my head. Recently, I was back in hospital for being danger to myself and all I could think about was if my stay would end before the West Indies-Bangladesh ODIs start.

After I got out, I called Bapi. After the initial exchanges, he asked, "Do you write for ESPN?" "You know how hard it is to get published," I replied.
"Oh" he said. "I love you."

I did not reply. In our culture it is a bit awkward to say something like that. But, I am saying it now:

I love you too, Bapi.

A Sepoy Silhouette (1845)

March 3, 1845

Sylhet and her rich heritage, a bustling town of mystics, of saints and Sufis, must have been a sight to behold in the late nineteenth century. For this town is also the home of Bangladesh's first recorded history of cricket. A fact which was otherwise surreptitiously kept secret from me when I visited a dak bungalow surrounded by lush tea gardens back in 2010.

So it is with great surprise when I was flipping the pages of The Illustrated History of Indian Cricket by Boria Majumdar I stumbled upon this curious fact when the word 'Bangladesh' stood out like an atheist in a room full of sorcerers. All credit do belong to the Bengal Rhodes Scholar for discovering the gem of scorecard from the murky depths of Sport Intelligence magazine in his research. It is turned out to be an intriguing story of Sepoys, on the mantle-shelf of Annals of Bangladesh cricket.

Let us now travel back to March 3, 1845 to the town where perhaps ekka, fiacre or gharry charioting through a bazaar, or by hillocks or jheels, or across the muddy roads with snakecharmers, or to be stopped by a parade of artillery troops of British East India company.

The British colonization of Indian subcontinent began in the eighteen century and the Company employed lascars and sepoys. Cricket was slowly gaining momentum and undergoing changes such as from underarm bowling to round arm one. The first match was played at The Oval on the same year. Now, the word sepoy comes from the Persian word, sipahi, which means soldier. One such sepoy was Sepoy Soophul whose bowling was "first rate in both matches" and That's about all that remains of the man's heroism on that day between European officers and the sepoys of the Light company against the other companies of 28th Regt. N.I. As Majumdar highlights about the reporter who:

"[...] goes on to single out Sepoy Lungum for his extraordinary batting prowess and declares that in a season or two, the native sepoys would be equipped to handle the best European cricket talent in the country."

And in another report entitled "Sepoy Cricket at Sylhet":

"...a second reporter writes that the match between two regimental sides, each containing no less than eight native cricketers, was perhaps the best contest encounter of the season."

Majumdar goes on to mention the blockbuster Hindi film Lagaan, which may have taken inspiration from such events as backdrop.

The anonymous author writing to the editor of The Englishman magazine, who was dubbed as A

WOULD-BE CRICKETER, describes further the genuine esprit de corps of the sepoys under Sepoy Cricketers! in the Intelligence:

"Indeed there seems a fair prospect of our having as good Cricketers among the sepoys of the Regiment in the course of another season or two, as are to be met with, judging from the various accounts of matches I have read of, among the Europeans in India. If the Cricketers at the several stations, would encourage the sepoys to join them; making allowances atfirst for their want of knowledge of the game, it would prove, if I mistake not, a very good means of improving one of the great defects so often complained of, the distance of the Europeans in the intercourse with the native. Several of the native, commissioned and non-commissioned officers of the Regiment, are in the habit of attending; one counts the overs, while another keeps the score; and the remainder act as lookers on; all appearing interested in the game. The European officers in the Regt. from the senior to the junior, who have leisure to do so, encourage the game either as spectators or players. Were they not to do so, notwithstanding the spirit in which it is now carried on, I fear the sepoys would not long continue to play."

As for the actual match, we can perhaps resurrect by modelling from scorecard. Light Company would bat first and in the first innings opener Captain Powell would get a duck. The rest of the runs are all in single digit column barring Sepoys Sungum Opudeale scoring 1-1-2-1-6 of 11 runs before being bowled by Salmon. Light Company would put up 37 on board as the Other Companies would be but to bat and dismissed for 59 with no one reaching double figures except 10 runs off byes.

In the second innings, Light Company would add 51 on board with Sepoy Roostum as top scorer of 14 runs while the Other Companies would go on to score 73 to end the "first record of a native cricket match".

Gone are the shadowy figures of Roostum, Soophul, Merwan Singh and others, but their spirit will forever be live on. Cricket at the end of the day is a strange tales of twists and turns rewarding only the purest seekers of them all. And I have been fortunate to be one such soul!

Colonel Brett's gallantry at Chittagong (1934)

This happened during Chittagong Uprising in the early 1930s. Surya Sen, leader of the rebels was hanged and the Hindu terrorists sought revenge by rounding off spectators during a cricket match. George_Cross

At teatime on Sunday January 7, 1934 about 50 European players and spectators, including women and children, were in the tea tent chatting and taking refreshment.At about 5.30 pm teatime an attack was suddenly made upon a group of European players and spectators by four youths armed with a revolver and seven bombs. The group included children and women and they were taken under a shamiana (tent) on a hillock and two assailants came out from behind a small bungalow and threw bombs running at the Europeans. Both the bombs were dud. As one was firing, Major Douglas Brett, unarmed, rushed to the man, wrestled him to the ground and saved the day from the terrorist.

Colonel is the only one man who has received a medal for bravery on the field of play. Subsequently he was awarded the Empire Gallantry Medal, later officially exchanged for the George Cross.

I believe this will keep you enchanted till tomorrow for about the gentleman who was never dismissed in his life, ended the Sadhu solemnly!

Sir Ash and the Strange Case of Mughal Bellboy

It was a chilly and windy morning in 122B Eskaton Road when my friend was sipping in his SadhaKalo branded mug of strong Arabica coffee and taking a pinch of herbal incense from his Bulgarian snuff-box and putting in a open cigar paper on which he did a surgery with a box-cutter. At precisely 1:58pm his session was interrupted by doorbell and soon Jamal, our *baburchi*, informed us that a head of a local club was here for *chadaa*.

Sir Ash, who had zero-tolerance for such matter, instructed Jamal to usher him in as he briefly patted his inner pocket of his mackintosh feeling for his 9mm Slovakian Grandpower revolver. Our attendant brought an albino gentleman charred from the summer's sun who was in his early 40s with burly hair, and had a *chador* wrapped around his body.

"Sir, ami kintu chadar jonnyo ashi ni..."

"I know," said Sir Ash in a steely, accent that hinted on near-about Mugdapara region. It was a while back, my friend authored a monograph on regional accents Shekhertek strip after living in the Japanese quarters in that region for 3 weeks. So it is not outside the whimsical nature of Sir Ash to experiment the different dialects he mastered which greatly abets his disguise.

But surprised I was, "By jove!" I cried out seeing Sir Ash make a dive toward the hapless man and with a flair of a showman make a hand-wave to pull-apart what happened to be a wig of our visitor announcing: "Amir, I present you-"

"Coach Siddons!!!" all three of us broke out, the visitor acknowledge his poorly constructed disguise.

"You see gentleman," my friend began to divulge "After studying local dialects, it was apparent from the start that no sane neighbor would be so bashful in his *shuddhyo bhasha*. You notice Amir although the words rolled out of his tongue effortlessly- no doubt a sheer 3 day rehearsal could be the due reason- but a local would more likely to spurt out a pronounced: "Ami kintoo chandaar lagi ai nai sir," instead of the polished: Sir ami kintoo chadar jonnyo ashi ni" as we pay extra attention to 'ni' in passing.

"Well Mr Siddons," he turned to the visitor who was by now sipping in green tea and *chanachur* brought by Jamal. "What can we do for you?"

"Sir Ash," who looked very apologetic for the abuse of his identity although it was *he* who was startled, "It was by no means by original idea to take refuge under such disguise had it not been because of constant pestering by many in the street who tries to exploit by semi-celebrity status. Also due to my foreign appearance I get accosted prematurely for occasional autographs. When I chanced upon the fact that you are do take kind to those who are ask *chaada* I thought of using reverse psychology..."

"Tut tut" my friend awkwardly cut him off. "But pray do tell us *why* you are here?"

"Lahore."

"Excuse me," Matin- sobriquet of the famous cricketer looked at me quizzically when I had equally blank expression he turned to the coach. "Please elaborate."

"The national cricket team would be playing a game in the neutral venue Gaddafi Stadium at Lahore against the Emirates in a week and we would need to beat them by a large margin. Also we believe the reputation of the country would be greatly enhanced if you contributed a stunning century."

"You do understand, adjectives as of that nature, "stunning" "large" are purely subjective Coach?" said the cricketer *sotto voce*.

"Yes, but Sir, we are desperate and we would need you to launch a showy performance. If you do plan on taking the case, we would be greatly obliged. Here are two tickets to Lahore for the Asia Cup opener. I hope you understand the value of it since it would be an opening match and we need to make a strong statement," as he paused for air he looked into the cricketer for desperation: "Sir?" "I will take the case."

We arrived the next day by *Biman* to Lahore and the cricketer wasted no time to start his investigation as he told the cab to take us directly to Gaddafi stadium. The stadium which is named after (now fallen) Libyan leader was designed by the architect Nayyar Ali Dada, who renovated the site in 1996.

The Mughal motif of red-bricks and arches is distinctive of the stadium. The lower portion was filled with shops and boutiques. It hosted the final of the World Cup 1996 and was first stadium in Pakistan to have floodlights. It is capable of seating 60,000 crowds and as I walked by the boundary rope taking in the whole scene of the empty lot and smelling the freshly mowed grass, Sir Ash printed out satellite images of the stadium and copiously took notes after coding a simulation of the topography of the stadium after inspecting the *anache-kanache* of the stadium with a powerful magnifying lens yet all the time toking on herbal incense from the joint.

As he talked to the groundsmen Sir Ash regaled us with history lessons that three hat-tricks have been committed on this ground by a Kiwi Peter Petherick against Pakistan on October 9, 1976, Washim (whom he referred solely as *Bhai* against Sri Lanka on March 6, 1999 Mohammad Sami of of Pakistan against Sri Lanka.

Next three days he would leave after breakfast and come back to our hotel late at night visibly exhausted. His industry fueled by whiskey (which he regularly managed from a local connect in the Islamic state) and incense started taking toll both on his cerebral and physical body and I could not help but sternly point it out and to seek both psychiatric and medical advise. But he took no caution instead pored over arcane abstracts in Artificial Intelligence journals in JSTOR.

Little did I know all his hard work would surreptitiously morph into a strange case that would not only earn him the reputation of a man of words but of highest dignity as well.

What followed on June 24, 2008 is nothing sort of a miracle.

As I woke up next day still stunned by the marvel which my friend produced after promising Coach Siddons of a century and living up to the innings which has invariably been dubbed as Eid-innings, I was a bit surprised to see the same pattern continue of a half-eaten scrambled egg and buttery toast on plate with Sir Ash missing. But I found a brief note under the table lamp which consisted of the eight words:

Meet me at Ambassador, 7 Davis Road

I hurriedly got off my pajamas and wore a jacket and half-ironed jeans and hailed a cab to take me to the destination. I was greeted by the valet whom I tipped some *rupiahs* and as I prompted the receptionist for Mr.Mohammad Ashraful a bell-boy appeared out of nowhere and told me in Urdu that apparently Sir Ash has been waiting for me for a long time and would gladly take me up to his room. Keeping up with the sub-continental culture and theme of the hotel the bell-boy was a 5'11" sturdy and fair *pathaan* in a garb of *sherwani* and *pagri* with silver studded wrist-cufflinks.

As he ushered me upto the fourth floor from the lobby I could not help but notice an awkward and almost unreal and subtly hostile vibes that the bell-boy was producing but nevertheless he knocked the door 2 times and upon no answer inserted his card and went inside.

I grew impatient at this strange twist of events and I was relieved to see my friend, himself, open the door and invite me in.

What I found was a messy interior where tomes and volumes ranging from diverse field such as mechanics, control theory, robotics, artificial intelligence littered everywhere as well as wallpapers scrawled with flow-charts, diagrams, and obscure mathematical formulas adorning everywhere which was eligible for writing.

"By Jove!" I yelled out. Immediately the whole reason behind his routine missing from dawn to dusk became apparent to me. It seemed he made an arrangement to check out books from University of Lahore primarily on control theory and as evident from the ashes of joints on the ashtrays, these have verily been keeping him quite busy for the last few days.

"But wait Ash-" in my excitement I forgot to address him properly "What of the mysterious bell boy?"

"Huh? What bell boy?"

"I swore he went inside the room." And frantically I began to search in vain as well as peer over the window which led to nothingness.

"Oh my dear Amir. You mean the late Jafar?" he jestfully proclaimed taking some chromium tubes in from a briefcase full of metal alloys, nuts, screw drivers, and LED.

"My friend it is with utmost sadness I announce that the Jafar is no longer with us."

"Sir Ash! But I don't understand!! What happened to him?? And what on God's name have you been doing here for all these days...and the books? What is of this strange obsession with mechanical objects the remnants of which.."

"More precisely *of whom*," corrected my friend.

And then everything became clear to me. "Is *THAT* so?"

A twinkle glimmered briefly in Sir Ash's eyes. He chuckled and acquiesced.

"Yes my dear Amir. Yes...what you see in that briefcase.."

"Is the remains of the bell-boy!" I cried out.

"*Exactement*," claimed the cricketer in flawless French accent. "My dear Amir, I present you Jafar," with an air of a conjuror he waved his hand over the suitcase and started to zip it shut. "But speak no more. Speak no more of this to anyone." And he launched on to explain in the monologue:

"You see ever since Coach approached me, I realized in order to cook up a century I need to create a perfect bowling machine. You may no doubt have heard of the chess playing Turkish automaton which was revealed to be a big hoax.

"So right after we arrived at Lahore the Mughal architecture of the stadium fueled my muse to create the perfect solution to the bowling attack of the UAE players. Thus I went on to labor prodigiously over each and everything I could find on automaton, robotics and artificial intelligence of whose brief glimpse you already got. After studying the bowling video tirelessly for hours I programmed Jafar to replicate the bowling attack of Arshad, Khurram, Zahid, Fahad and the rest of the gang of the Emirates. Finally I reached a stage where I could pass the automaton as near-human after I programmed it to get a job as a bell-boy in Ambassador hotel. Now, if you follow me to the window you would see that behind the thicket of the bougainvillea shades by the gazebo there is an archway over a path. The path leads straight to a deserted field where I tirelessly practiced playing deliveries for 12 hours a day as the Jafar would mimic all the pacers down to their details and the spinner to the finest nuance."

"My God!" as I looked around he also reminded me that his innings consisted of not a single six which greatly increased his chances of cutting down aerial shots as well as his game elevated an otherwise Raqibul of different character to take full advantage of powerplay. Undoubtedly their partnership with was aided by the century from Jafar's bowling as well as reaching the 300 mark helped accomplish his task.

"But not a second to waste," said Sir Ash.

"Wait...you needed to have considerable amount of money to pay. Where did you manage that?"

"That..that was possible through Coach Siddons' advance of 500,000 US dollars. But Amir...we need to erase all evidence and prepare for Sri Lanka!"

Welcome to the Circus Act!

Hulloh! Calling all my fellow Englishmen, greenhorn and alderman, from yokels 'n bumpins to flue-flakers 'n Parish prig...Welcome to the Circus Act! Forget the Piccadilly Circus, grab yur fish`n chips, roll down yur hackney, put'on yur hock-dockeys `cuz circus is in town. Yesssirree Bob...and Jack. We got a circus full of act with jack-pudding 'n merry andrews awaiting to pull the biggest gag you yet to ever have.

First I present you with a lad. Oh what's so special about him you say? Ay. He is a prodigy.

Prodigy, hein? Oh, he aint not just your ordinary boy genius! Oh no, no! Forget your Hampdenshire Wonder or the Lubeck prodigy. This one here scored a test century at the youngest age. Ay that's right. Look more into the mirror. Image in the mirror shows the past of a man who is now wayy past his puberty having his many shares of last laughs behind the tears of a clown.

Next I present you not just any ordinary stilt-walker, ay, but a man of such towering heights that he is the only man of his kind (and one of the top ten in the world) to reach the height of 150 mark with his towering sixes that makes Big Ben look like a monopoly house. Tell yu what bloke here capable of setting the Thames on fire on any given day. Pour in the shillings....pence two pence aye fill up my pewter....cuz now I bring you..

Mr.Jack-of-all-Trades. At about 1.7 meters , weighing roughly 10 stones or 4.6 slugs behind the joker's white makeup, always smiling, often dubbed as the Smiling Assassin, this man is not only is a jack-of-all-trades but sure is master of many. He is given the title for being the best at what he does by honorific Committee. He is number one all-rounder, #3 ODI bowler, #3 Test all-rounder. What more talent can you ask from a man? He is a puppeteer pulling the strings of the team, a ventriloquist who is the voice of Bd cricket, a silent mime who is louder in action. Now one helluva talented pierrot!

Arightie nib-cove...that oughta be enough for 'ntatainment, ey? But hold on! We got more, we have two Loki like trixsters who can pull magic tricks out of their hats, so that gives you five already. Who are they you say? Ay they go by the name "Aloukik" and "Raj." Yup, these two 'ere 'ill have ya in yar knickerbockers by performing vanishing act of yar wickets three-in-a-row on any given day...

Now then we already got five of a kind, I produce you two more in one breath. One is one of handful of fastest slinger alive, who can shoot faster than a man in cannonball, who is an express delivery man and the other wildcard is one of the handful of five who scored six sixes in six balls. Yclept Chokka Naeem 'dis devil...nah 'dis gremlin 'ere rolls on the very wheel of death.

Hulloh! What do we have there? Two stubborn fellas. Ay. I unveil Mr. Old Keebler. Mr. Old Keebler has been dubbed the chatterbox cuz of his non-stopping chatter. Mr Keeble here who sits on his knees most of his days and is a part time juggler who will drop anythin but a mug full of rumsy. He is know for his fastest maiden test century against the #1 side now. And a man just like him, who has been dubbed as Bangladesh's Peter Pan is.... Mohammad Mahmadulluh, a harlequin whose forte always seems to be when no one seems to be doing their act, he comes at the last minute and saves the nation, with tons or semi-tons out of thin air. Imagine him doing a balance act of seven men above him, an atlas who carries a load of collapse over his shoulder, he literally puts the map on Bangladesh.

As the acrobats followed by Zunaed, Kayes, Nafees comes, I produce one of a kind part-time hand-balancer, who can beat the strongest of lads in one-handed pushup, billed as one of the best new ball bowlers, not a unicyclist but an express train, who is worth a whoppin 600k....Com'un! Com'un...for two fortnights only, rain or shine, I present you with one of a kinda circus with breads for munchin'...'urry ma booboisies..'urry!...

Forget Imaginarium of Doctor Parnassus, you are about to see the greatest show in the world!

Weird coincidences between Einstein and Ashraful

I found them really spooky. Hope you like them.

    Both Einstein and Ashraful contains 8 letters.
    Einstein's miracle year: 1905. Ashraful's Eid innings in Cardiff: 2005. Exactly 100 years later.
    Einstein's first publication: 1901. Ashraful's test debut: 2001. Exactly 100 years later.
    Einstein was 76 years old. Ashraful is 26 years old. Difference of exactly 50 years.
    Einstein was more of an intuitionist; Ashraful known for natural game.
    Both worked with spin. Einstein spin of a particle in Bose-Einstein condensate, while Ash delved heavily into spinning of a ball.
    Both are known for being absentminded or careless.

    Both are obsessed with numbers. Einstein loved maths while Ashraful would have been a statistician in another life. (source: Firdose Moonda).
    Both are known for being slow learners or having speech difficulty.
    Einstein as a child envisioned riding over a beam of light. Ash is compared to 'ball of fire'.
    Einstein said: "Anyone who has never made a mistake has never tried anything new." Ashraful believes the same thing.
    Both possesses valuable medal. Einstein received Copley Medal. Ashraful, Gold Medal in Guangzhou in 2010.
    Einstein published over 150 non-scientific works, while Ashraful scored over 150 -his highest in Test.
    Both are heavily involved with gravitational work.
    Both owned several copies of the same dress. Einstein had black suits while Ashraful similar jerseys.
    Both lived in flat. Both are known for flamboyant self-expression: Einstein with outstretched tongue photo while Ashraful with dance.
    Both failed university entrance exam.
    There is a restaurant by Einstein's name, while Ashraful owns his own restaurant.
    Both are considered genius in their respective fields.

A Shakespearean Tragedy (Day 1 of Test 2: Bangladesh v India)

Act I Scene I
Enter Sehwag
Sehwag:
You are not worth the dust which the rude wind
Blows in your face.

Dhoni:
"'Tis best to weigh
The enemy more mighty than he seems.

Act II Scene I
Enter Lotus Kamal

Lotus Kamal:
"How sharper than a serpent's tooth it is to have a thankless child!"

Shakib:
"O villain, villain, smiling, damned villain!"
Act II Scene I

Commentators: Game's
afoot!

After Imrul gets out by a bad decision.
Billy Bowden: Fair is foul, and foul is fair.

Tamim muses after he gets out:
"Methinks sometimes I have no more wit
than a Christian or an ordinary man has:
but I am a great eater of beef
and I believe that does harm to my wit." [pause]

"What day is day, night night, and time is time,
Were nothing but to waste night, day, and time;
Therefore, since brevity is the soul of wit,
And tediousness the limbs and outward flourishes,
I will be brief. Your noble son is mad. . . ."

"Parting is such sweet sorrow, that I shall say good night till it be morrow." Junaid at the other end:

Ashraful arrives...

Sehwag seeing the scorecard: "Lord,
what fools these mortals be!"

Ashraful:
"And worse I may be yet: the worst is not,
So long as we can say, This
is the worst."

He too gets out

Ashraful:
"Better a witty fool than a foolish wit." [pause]
"I dare do all that may become a man;
Who dares do more, is none."

Exeuent Ashraful

Shakib in disgust:
Our separation so abides and flies That thou,
residing here, goes yet with me, And I, hence
fleeting, here remain with thee. Away!

Athar Ali Khan:
"If this were play'd upon a stage now, I could condemn it as an improbable fiction."

Siddons:
[Aside] Though this be madness, yet there is method in't. [pause] "We
know what we are, but know not what we may become."

Sunil Gavaskar on Ashraful:
"Nothing in his life
Became him like the leaving it; he died
As one that had been studied in his death,
To throw away the dearest thing he ow'd,
As 'twere a careless trifle." [pause]

What's done can't be undone.

Shiva:
"To climb steep hills requires slow pace at first."

Roqibul:
"Time ... thou ceaseless lackey to eternity."

Shamim Chowdhury:
"I will praise any man that will praise me."

Shakib:
Is this her fault or mine?
The tempter or the tempted, who sins most? Ha!
Not she; nor doth she tempt; but it is I
That, lying by the violet in the sun, Do as
the carrion does, not as the flower,
Corrupt with virtuous season.

Shakib nicks one to Dhoni

Zaheer Khan gleefully
"O cunning enemy, that, to catch a saint,
With saints dost bait thy hook!"

Shakib:
"Most dangerous
Is that temptation that doth goad us on
To sin in loving nature."

Shakib soliloquoy (on his shot selection):
"To be, or not to be: that is the question:
Whether 'tis nobler in the mind to suffer
The slings and arrows of outrageous fortune, Or
to take arms against a sea of troubles,
And by opposing end them? To die: to sleep;
No more; and by a sleep to say we end
The heart-ache and the thousand natural shocks
That flesh is heir to, 'tis a consummation
Devoutly to be wish'd. To die, to sleep;
To sleep: perchance to dream: ay, there's the rub;
For in that sleep of death what dreams may come When
we have shuffled off this mortal coil."

Twelfth man of BD walks in:

"O! what a rogue and peasant slave am I!"

Mahmudullah Riyad (at the middle of his master
innings) "I and my sword will earn our chronicle." Walks
up to his partner....
"Let not the piece of virtue which is set
Betwixt us, as the cement of our love
To keep it builded, be the ram to batter
The fortress of it. For better might we
Have loved without this mean, if on both parts
This not be cherished."

Mushfiq walks in.
An Indian player:
Look like the innocent flower,
But be the serpent under it.

Mushfiqur:
To-morrow, and to-morrow, and to-morrow,
Creeps in this petty pace from day to day,
To the last syllable of recorded time; And all
our yesterdays have lighted fools The way to
dusty death. Out, out, brief candle!
Life's but a walking shadow, a poor player,
That struts and frets his hour upon the stage,
And then is heard no more. It is a tale
Told by an idiot, full of sound and fury,
Signifying nothing.

Zaheer Khan:

When maidens sue,
Men give like gods; but when they weep and kneel,
All their petitions are as freely theirs
As they themselves would owe them.

"When beggars die there are no comets seen;
The heavens themselves blaze forth the death of princes." -Shafiul laments after his dismissal

Dhoni [Aside]

"Why then tonight let us assay our plot."

"Wisely and slow; they stumble that run fast". -commentator Shiva as Rubel almost runs out Riyad

Sunny on stadium crowd before Riyad's anticipated century:
There is a tide in the affairs of men.
Which, taken at the flood, leads on to fortune;
Omitted, all the voyage of their life Is bound
in shallows and in miseries.
On such a full sea are we now afloat, And we
must take the current when it serves, Or lose
our ventures.

"As he was valiant, I honour him. But as he was ambitious, I slew him." -Harbhajan Singh after bowling out Rubel

"Beware the ides of March." -England captain Cook warns about the forthcoming tour

"The rest is silence"

Profile of The Deranged Acrobat

The traits of a glovesman vary. His trace has to be invisible. For instance, take the strange cases of Probir Sen at Cuttack taking the hat-trick in First Class cricket against Orissa in the 1954-55 season; or A.C.Smith for that matter who was guilty of it in 1965 versus Essex at Clacton playing for Warwickshire.

Both of these men share the distinction of having carved a niche of being the only wicketkeepers to have achieved such a feat. Add to that the fact that A.C.Smith was a front-line bowler.

Legends and lore further mention the story of Alan Knott, unarguably one of the greats, if not the greatest, who put meat steaks or plasticine in his gloves for cushioning purposes. Knott also used to roll down his sleeves to protect his elbow from bruises while diving and warm his hands with hot water before every match. In addition, part of his curriculum included giving catches in the shower over the partition in the cubicle to catch the other person off-guard.

Such men have gone to great lengths. The character is rich and varied. Some are plain and outright brutal like Adam Gilchrist, who like a zamburak perched on a camel shoots billboards and balustrades and floodlights and fuselages. Randomly pick and read any chapter out of his Vedantic sagas in the IPL and he won't fail to surprise you.

Adam Gilchrist has the best figures, stats-wise, for a wicket-keeper in International cricket. Compare his 472 wickets at a dismissal per innings ratio of 1.679 with our Golden Protege's 101 dismissals of 71 catches and 31 stumpings at a ratio of 0.990. But before the reader turns away in aghast looking at the contrast thinking he may not be in the same tier as the Dhonis, Sangakkaras and Bouchers, I offer this gem of his flash of insight for his inclusion in the team:

Our friends from the sister asylum once quoth:

> 7.1 Abdur Razzak to Prior, 1 wide, OUT, gone! What a bizarre dismissal, Prior has had a brain fade. It drifted down the leg side, Prior missed it and drags his back foot. Rahim takes off the bails and Prior is just safe, but then he stays out of his crease and Rahim shows brilliant awareness to pull the stump out of the ground to complete the stumping a second time. Brainless from Prior, superb from Rahim
>
> MJ Prior st â€ Mushfiqur Rahim b Abdur Razzak 15 (35m 20b 2x4 0x6) SR: 75.00

Yes, Mushfiqur may not have used meat steaks for cushion but he did show his anticipatory capability with this kinematic flash of witticism. I say we still persist with him as our keeper. Mushfiqur celebrates dismissal

At 5 feet 4, the 'chatterbox' from Bogra seems to have the X factor. His motivation like a squirrel on amphetamine can relentlessly energize his team and his solid partnerships involving the constant rotation of strike speak for themselves. On the flip side, I do concede his captaincy has been shoddy sometimes, failing to rotate the right combo of bowlers and strangle the opponent at the right time. Ah yes, the way he gave away byes in the third ODI against Pakistan last night, triggered our very own member "bujhee kom" to astutely point out that perhaps he needs a backup wicketkeeper.

But didn't he also take the ball between his knee to get rid of a batsman once? Mushfiqur recently has been at the receiving end with an Atlas-like burden of the captain's role. Give him some time I say. Meanwhile, the 100 and 101st wickets that he helped take in tandem with Riyad did set up a could-be hat-trick scenario. Plus, readers won't be nonplussed to know he has a perfect rapport with his vice-captain as well as aiding and abetting in valuable partnerships.

The role of a wicketkeeper-captain is so rich that he must also consistently brainstorm to make bowling revisions, swap bowlers at bowling ends, set up the "perfect" field, be literally quick on his feet and stand up to batsmen.

Sledging is a natural tenet of wicket keepers that comes with the territory and although often times, Mushfiqur's exuberance can pierce through stump microphones, he lacks Healy-McCullum genes to get under the opponent's skin through verbal gymnastics. Groomed to be obedient and polite, Bangladeshis are often held in high esteem for being model citizens, but banters can be naive, harmless and still unsettle a batsman. If garrulous Mushfiqur must be, then fashion it in a psychological trap of a havoc of cacophony.

However neat and tidy may his stunt-double Dhiman be, Mushfiqur still deserves to play the key role. The sacerdotal anecdotal feat of Mushfiqur reaching his milestone could be swept under the rug as this same man has been victim of yet another record - a world record at that - of conceding most byes before the 16th over. Yet, I still weigh in favor of his role in spite of isolated instances of dropped catches and missed stumpings, or failure to read the ball on numerous occasions.

Mushfiqur's journey has just begun. He needs to quadruple his efforts if he wants to carve his name in history as the greatest keeper that ever lived. He has shown rare glimpses of neurons firing and he is a leader. All the ingredients are there, all he needs is the surge to evolve into a ruthless character.

As the scullery spoke : A personal review of the first day (West Indies tour, 2012)

Once a twelve year old housemaid in charge of scullery and other minor chores of our Banani apartment remarked that Tamim hit a first-ball six at Lord's. It wouldn't be till last week that I would see the fault in his schizophrenic imagination on Youtube when rewinding the English innings of what seemed to be a six but a pull for four. But some imaginative prowess it is!

I am a spiritual person and God doesn't care who or what should be His mouthpiece. It wasn't till last now that I saw how the dots connected to fruition his imagination to reality when Christopher Gayle would make yet another bizarre World Record of being the only sentient being to hit a firstball six in Test since it's inception at MCG in 1877.

Gayle certainly took to his ego when he was greeted with a newly capped Sohag Gazi clubbing him for two sixes and four byes netting a whopping 18 runs in the opening over. Well, Mushfiq would persist with the bowler who kept bowling flighted deliveries as Gayle himself would be the victim of one such delivery to Mahmudullah at long-off but not till scoring 24 off 17 at a strike rate 141.17. Celebrating first wicket.

In spite of the later tons by Chanderpaul and Powell, the shot of the day still remains the straight drive from Gayle at fourth over off Rajib down the wicket timed to sweet perfection and minimal effort.

Perhaps Shamim Chowdhury's delight to see his forecast come true is noteworthy while we are discussing eerie coincidences. Right after he mused to his fellow commentator that BD players might pull a quick one out of nowhere after minutes of resistance, a wicket would instantly manifest.

Apart from the bizarre Gayle record and the dead-ball wicket which resulted after a ball got kicked out off Riyad's helmet to the spectacular hands of Rubel, this match would be special for me for being the dreamy vision of a hitting the first six of a Test ball as foretold by a scullion.

Close Encounter of the Last Kind

Danish American social reformer Jacob August Riis said the following:

Look at a stone cutter hammering away at his rock, perhaps a hundred times without as much as a crack showing in it. Yet at the hundred-and-first blow it will split in two, and I know it was not the last blow that did it, but all that had gone before.

And what else encapsulates this hypothesis better than the Tiger's road to victory from brink of disasters, losses and whitewashes over and over...

Rewind back to October 18, 2008. Exactly two years ago having beaten New Zealand in the first ODI ever, Bangladesh kicks off the test in Chittagong. Cricinfo proudly proclaims "Shakib leaves New Zealand in tatters" and surely he does having scalped 6 wickets for 31 runs off 24 overs leaving the Kiwis stuttering at 155 for 9 trailing Bangladesh for 90 runs. Surely victory is in sight? Alas! Clotho yet to shape the destiny for Tigers.

Further walk back down the memory lane. June 28, 2008. India versus Bangladesh showdown in Asia Cup at Karachi. Leopard man Alok Kapali - the first man ever to tattoo his name in history with a century against India for his country - helps pile on a massive score of 283 abetted by his partner in crime Tamim Iqbal's quickfire 55. As Karachi rains with Kapalis sixes, even Arun Lal in commentary box chimes out that India better do something about it as the game is getting away from them. Sprinkle in the dew factor to the mammoth total and surely you have victory in sight? Alas! "Bangladesh stuck in what-if phase!" Lachesis yet to smile.Â

Fast forward to January 16, 2009. Months have passed. The team kept on grinding in the duration. Suddenly Bangladesh beats Sri Lanka with a thunderous 92 from Shakib in a rain curtailed Duckworth-Lewis gunning down the target and taking the team to the final versus Sri Lanka for a sniff of first ever series victory. And guess what? Even after posting a measly 152 in dead rubber at Mirpur, bowlers topple the top order committing a gruesome mess of 6 for 5. Atrophied pitch, trophy sure to belong to the Tigers in a historic series win....Alas! only to be checked by Atropos, the last of the Moirae, who spins the game on it's head in a volte-face from the vim and vigor of Murali's bludgeoning Rubel to victory.

And thus the pattern continues. Or rather did-- till the recent series win of the Tigers versus the Blackcaps. Gods have smiled, sacrifices made, thousands of expatriate fans' vigil have been answered all leading up to the grand finale for the ultimate feast in Valhalla.

Not even Hollywood could have written a better script.

Weird and Wonderful Ways to Improve our Cricket

Here's my 2 cents of armchair theorizing...

Batsmen should go out in the field and score 24 and after that MUST GET OUT!! I don't care if it was the fastest ever 24 (like four 6s) and how brilliantly he batted, he should either retire, hit wicket or give catching practise to the fielders. In that way, we will have 24X10= 240 score. Of course, the tail enders need to have work cut out. Reason? There would be no psychological pressure whatsoever because each batsmen will go out in the field knowing that he has to score ONLY 24 runs and that he is playing the role of a mere chum in a grander scheme of life instead of being a hero. Reduced ego, more teamwork will yield effortless scoring of 24runs after consistency of 10 matches straight.

Latch into Twenty20 mode. Who says we have to play ALL 50 overs? We have seen how easily a team can score roundaobut 200 in 20 overs. Benefits? Say we do manage to get into a fiery, aggressive, scourge-of-God T20 mode and do score 200 in 20 overs losing all our wickets, will have more energy because we didn't trundle along for 50 overs stretch, whilst our opponents will have a different gameplan...

Say a bowler bowls 5 balls conceding several ordinary runs. Then all of a sudden he switches into a bizarre form of cricket. He deliberately bowls all wides in the leg side- infact so much wider that batsmen wouldnt even able to reach it much as he tries. Not only this the bowler continues this lunacy for say 13 more balls. All wides. And then all of a sudden just when the batsmen is out of his comfort zone, getting in the groove lulled into a false sense of pattern, the genius bowler bowls a dead-on straight ball catching him so off guard that either he is lbw-ed or clean bowled. Sure he may concede like 13 runs, but it's a sacrifice just like chess. Queen's Gambit Declined? I dont think so.

"Limp bowling": you know how we bowl to infants when we are just playing. Sooo softly, sooo smoothly inviting him to hit. Apply the same principle. Don't even try to bowl. Is he gonna hit 6s or 4s everytime? I dont care if he's Dhoni or Afridi or Symonds, how long will he be able to carry this on? This would be a test of the batsman's tempermant n patience. At one point he will budge and reveal his weakness.

Score the fastest 50. All the target should be to amass this in the quickest way possible, and the hell if match goes downhill from then. Result? Say after this stretch of lunacy ends after few matches, the openers wouldn't experiment it anymore but would come out with the added sense of confidence "we can, but won't" mentality. End to paranoia. Heck this would even give a character of much needed smugness in our players.

What if the point of a cricket match is to lose it not win? Can we still 'win' meaning lose? If so, how badly can we actually lose? Maybe all out for 15? Or concede like 700 runs? Make all the records of lowest score, or highest total of opponents w/out a single wicket.

When you have lost everything in life, when you have nothing there is to lose, then you have nothing to fear. Have you ever seen Fight Club? You have nothing to lose, no shame, no guilt, you are stripped to a humilty of naked truth and then?...then you start from the scratch. You begin anew. It's like the rags-to- riches millionaire who has no fear cuz he has hit rock bottom in his life and even if his life were to turn upside down next day, he knows...he just knows he would make it someday. Same philosophy. Heck, even the sage Lao-Tsu would say: "Those who have nothing, have everything."

Make our star players refrain from sex and masturbation for 4 months straight and channel all the repressed sexual energy and aggression in smooth controlled manner in the field- much like what the boxers do...

No wicketkeeper. But the slow bowler must make sure of not leaking out any byes. And should just aim for the wickets only. Positives? Extra fielder on the other side but most importantly we wil have a batsman not fatigued from overworking by kneeling too much in the field.

All players wear helmet. Mainly to give the impression to the opponents that they are playing against a team who are fresh out of Bedlam, and who dont give a f---.

Strap the fielders to biofeedback when not playing to make them slow down their heart-rate and breathing so as to slow their perception of time, in order to perform superior fielding.

Practise telelpathy. There are certain websites in the net that allows you to predict what the next Zenner card would be and tests the level of your intuition.

Intentionally bar the spectators from coming to the stadium. It would be a sorry sight indeed! In fact, no coverage of any game. They should just play for the love of the game and not for any glory or fame or money.

Complete polar opposite of the previous one. Huge crowd. Instruct the audience to make ballyhoo n tantrum or Boo just at the moment a batsman is about to hit a ball. Hey! It works in basketball, the whole home court advantage deal.

Deliberately play with a player short.

Sheer insanity. Put all the 9 players on one side either leg or off. Just to bhorkaye dewar jonno. Umm...of course this may not possible cuz I am kinda uninitiated about the rules and regulations of a match.

Sheer madness. How about a runup for our bowler right from the pavilion end just before the boundary rope?

Silly point of our team smelling horribly bad so that the opposing batsmen cannot concentrate.

Intentionally get not one but two runners just to confuse the bowling side.

Subliminal adversiting all over the place in all the signs and billboards thereby programming the subconscious mind of the adversaries to lose while at the same time empowering the entire psyche our team with hidden positive messages.

Entire fielding side starts an uncontrollable guffaw all at the same time. No. They are not laughing at them but just happy to stay alive. Nothing in the rule book says a team cant give out 'ottohashi', does it? Nothing more than reaching the psychological abyss of the opposing batsmen to "vorkaye dewa" guiling them to think they are playing a bunch of jokers.

Playing against our minnows ONLY. Ireland, Kenya, Hong Kong, The Netherlands, UAE, Zimbabwe. Even the best lumberjack in the village needs sharpening their saw. At least, you can always flex your muscle of mastery and surpass yourself over and over till you finetune all your abilties. Why else do you think the other great team plays against us? Sure we can score 300, but why not target 400 agains the minnows? Why not strive to bowl them under 50 runs? Just test our level of skills and master. Besides...it does look damn good on our resume and record books.

Of course, no one would wanna take us seriously after this. S--- might even get our ODI status revoked for making mockery out of the game. But who cares? We got nothing to lose. Might as well just have fun in the field and control it by playing the way we want and not how our opponents want us to play...

"Though this be madness, yet there is method in't." - William Shakespeare
"Even a stopped clock is right twice a day." -Proverb

Ashraful never gets out...

Ashraful never got out. His average is infinity. He merely gave optical illusion that he is getting out to put some sanity in what would otherwise would have been total lunacy.

Ashraful was once a runner for two batsman.

A kid once complained Ashraful how he has no friends to play with. So he showed the kid how to bowl, bat and field all at the same time.

Once Shoaib Aktar broke Ashraful's bat. Three years later Shoaib got genital warts.

People confuses Ashraful with Shiva because he seems to have more than four hands when he fields.

Euler-Mascheroni constant was renamed after Ashraful to include figures from computing number of times Ashraful faced a ball + minutes Ashraful spent on field divided by runs he made with triple consecutive sixes.

When Ashraful throws a ball, it doesn't follow parabola but the ball invents a complex, hyperbolic, trajectory in higher dimension to find the most efficient route from point A to point B. Ashraful once hit a six and thwarted a federal bank robbery by knocking out goons with his ball. When Ashraful was given out later confirmed by snicko, he took up electrical engineering, got a phd and found a fault in the emf of the device.

Ashraful umpires his own match.

Ashraful chooses tail in double sided coin with heads and STILL wins.

Ashraful can paddle scoop underarm bowl....AND hit six.

Ashraful owns copyright to the word 'obviously' and receives 30% royalty check based on it's usage.

Humans persistence of vision is 24 frames per second...not enough to perceive Ashraful's slow medium right arm spin.

There are no boundary ropes for Ashraful....only event horizon.

The tradition that bowlers bowl from opposing ends started when Ashraful refused to move from the crease at the end of the over so the whole team shifted their position.

Lousiana celebrates Ash Wednesday after him.

Ashraful once hit six sixes of six different balls as the balls were never retrieved.

Printed in Dunstable, United Kingdom